Building SPELLING Skills — Grade 1 — Daily Practice

What's in This Book?

This 30-unit book contains strategies and practice for learning 198 spelling words.

Each unit contains:

- a list of spelling words (five in lists 1–14; eight in lists 15–30)
- one or two sentences for dictation
- four activity pages for practicing the spelling words

Words on the spelling lists were selected from:

- a list of the 200 most commonly used words in English
- words frequently misspelled by first-graders
- words with common phonetic elements
- words changed by adding endings

Additional resources:

- "How to Study" chart
- "Spelling Strategies" chart
- forms for testing and recordkeeping

Correlated to State Standards

Visit *www.teaching-standards.com* to view a correlation of this book's activities to your state's standards. This is a free service.

EMC 2705

Evan-Moor EDUCATIONAL PUBLISHERS
Helping Children Learn since 1979

Authors: Sharman and Douglas Wurst
Editor: Leslie Sorg
Copy Editor: Cathy Harber
Illustrator: Jim Palmer
Desktop: Jia-Fang Eubanks
Yuki Meyer

M000214599

Contents

Teaching the Weekly Unit

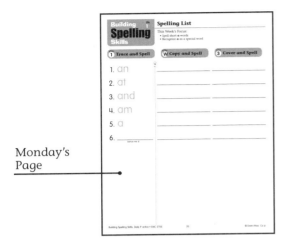

Monday's Page

Strengthening Students' Spelling Skills

Spelling Strategies
Page 6

How to Study Your List
Page 7

At the beginning of the year, reproduce pages 6 and 7 for each student or on an overhead transparency. Review the general steps and strategies, encouraging students to apply them throughout the year.

Monday

Allot ample class time each Monday for introducing the spelling list and having students complete the first page of the unit.

Introducing the Week's Words

Give each student the spelling list for the week. Here are ways to introduce the words:

- Call attention to important consistencies noted in "This Week's Focus," such as a phonetic or structural element. For example, say: *As we read this week's spelling list, notice that all the words have the same vowel sound.*

- Read each word aloud and have students repeat it.

- Provide a model sentence using the word. Have several students give their own sentences.

- If desired, add "bonus words" based on the needs of your class. These may be high-utility words or words that the class is encountering in curricular studies.

Writing the Words

After introducing the words, have students study and write the words on the first page of the unit, following these steps:

Step 1: Trace and Spell
Have students trace the word and spell it aloud.

Step 2: Copy and Spell
Tell students to copy the word onto the first blank line and spell it again, touching each letter as it is spoken.

Step 3: Cover and Spell
Have students fold the paper along the fold line to cover the spelling words so that only the last column shows. Then have students write the word from memory.

Step 4: Uncover and Check
Tell students to open the paper and check the spelling. Students should touch each letter of the word as they spell it aloud.

Home Connection

Send home a copy of the Parent Letter (page 145) and the Take-Home Spelling List for the week (pages 10–19).

Tuesday — Visual Memory Activities

Have students complete the activities on the second page of the unit. Depending on students' abilities, these activities may be completed as a group or independently.

Wednesday — Word Meaning and Dictation

Have students complete the Word Meaning activity on the third page of the unit. Then use the dictation sentences on pages 8 and 9 to guide students through "My Spelling Dictation." Follow these steps:

1. Ask students to listen to the complete sentence as you read it.

2. Say the sentence in phrases, repeating each phrase one time clearly. Have students repeat the phrase.

3. Wait as students write the phrase.

4. When the whole sentence has been written, read it again, having students touch each word as you say it.

Thursday — Word Study Activities

Have students complete the activities on the fourth page. Depending on students' abilities, these activities may be completed as a group or independently.

Friday — Weekly Test

Friday provides students the chance to take the final test and to retake the dictation they did on Wednesday. A reproducible test form is provided on page 142. After the test, students can record their score on the "My Spelling Record" form (page 141).

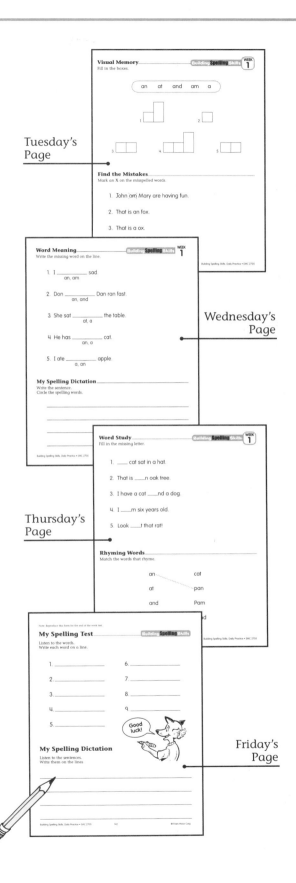

Tuesday's Page

Wednesday's Page

Thursday's Page

Friday's Page

Spelling Strategies

▶ Say a word correctly.

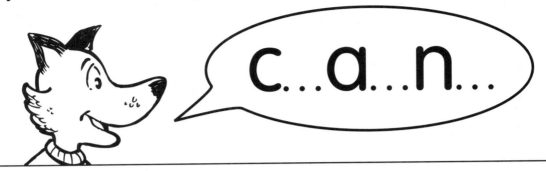

▶ Think about what the word looks like.

▶ Look for small words in spelling words.

▶ Use rhyming words to help spell a word.

6

How to Study Your List

❶ Trace and Spell

❷ Copy and Spell

❸ Cover and Spell

❹ Uncover and Check

Good for me!

Sentences for Dictation

There are one or two dictation sentences for each spelling list. Space for sentence dictation is provided on Wednesday of each week and on Friday's test form (page 142).

- Ask students to listen to the complete sentence as you read it.
- Have students repeat the sentence.
- Read the sentence in phrases, repeating each phrase one time clearly.
- Have students repeat the phrase.
- Allow time for students to write the phrase.
- Read the sentence again, having students touch each word as you say it.

Week	Dictation Sentences
1	I **am** on **a** bus.
2	**It is big**.
3	A **cat sat** in a **pan**.
4	**Six** cats and a man **ran**.
5	Is it **fun to run**?
6	**I** have a **pup** on the **bus**.
7	Is that **his** cat in the **sun**?
8	**The dog got on the** bus.
9	**Let** my **pet get fed**.
10	Did the **men stop** the **top**?
11	I put my **hand** in the **hot sand**.
12	The **cats** and **pigs** are in their **beds**.
13	The **ball fell** down the **hill**.
14	**She** saw a **shell** in the **dish**.
15	**Come** play the **game** by the **lake**.
16	I can **ride nine times** for a **dime**. **My five** cats are **by** the door.

Week	Dictation Sentences

17   That **bike** by the **gate** is **mine**.
I will **bake** a **fine** cake.

18   **He** can **see** the **sheep** by the **tree**.
We need to **be** at the game.

19   The **note** said to **go home**.
Do you have a **robe**?

20   I **gave** my **snake** a **late** lunch.
I can **use** my **feet** to make a **line**.

21   The **bees** were in the **boxes** of **roses**.
The **foxes** ate **bones**.

22   The **ant went** to **find** food.
I **want** to be **kind**.

23   Did **most** of the birds fly **fast** to the **nest**?
This **must** be the **last stamp**.

24   **May** I **play** with the **boat**?
Wear a **coat** when the **day** is cold.

25   Can you **smell** the **small** skunk by the **wall**?
All of us **will call** down the **well**.

26   Will you take the **brown cow** to **town**?
Now show me how to **row**.

27   **Are** you driving the **car far**?
At our **farm**, we put a **star** on each **jar** of jam.

28   The **funny bunny** jumped over the **puppy**.
The **happy little kitten** had a white **mitten**.

29   I **saw** a **paw** print on the **lawn**.
Did the **fawn** run and **then** stop?

30   **Take** a **look** at this **good book**.
I **took** some **wood** to make a **stand**.

Building Spelling Skills

Building **Spelling** Skills	
NAME	**WEEK 1**

an

at

and

am

a

_____
bonus word

Building **Spelling** Skills	
NAME	**WEEK 2**

in

is

it

big

did

_____
bonus word

Building **Spelling** Skills	
NAME	**WEEK 3**

can

pan

man

cat

sat

_____
bonus word

cut

cut

NAME

as

had

sit

six

ran

_____

bonus word

NAME

up

us

run

fun

to

_____

bonus word

cut

NAME

pup

bus

but

tub

I

_____

bonus word

cut

his

dig

pat

sun

put

_____
bonus word

not

on

dog

got

the

_____
bonus word

pet

get

let

fed

red

_____
bonus word

cut

cut

Building Spelling Skills

WEEK 10

top
stop
men
fix
fox

_____
bonus word

Building Spelling Skills

NAME

WEEK 11

ten
hat
hot
sand
hand

_____
bonus word

Building Spelling Skills

NAME

WEEK 12

cats
pigs
beds
bugs
tops

_____
bonus word

© Evan-Moor Corp. • EMC 2705

© Evan-Moor Corp. • EMC 2705

© Evan-Moor Corp. • EMC 2705

hill

bell

fell

ball

fall

_____
bonus word

she

ship

shell

dish

wish

_____
bonus word

make

came

lake

game

shake

ate

tape

come

_____
bonus word

five	gate	we
time	rake	me
like	name	he
dime	bake	be
ride	fine	see
nine	bike	need
my	hide	tree
by	mine	sheep

_____   _____   _____

bonus word   bonus word   bonus word

cut

cut

go

so

no

home

note

robe

do

you

_____
bonus word

late

gave

cone

line

snake

feet

jeep

use

_____
bonus word

ropes

bones

kites

bees

cakes

boxes

foxes

roses

_____
bonus word

cut

cut

went

sent

ant

bend

find

mind

kind

want

_____
bonus word

fast

last

nest

must

most

step

stamp

still

_____
bonus word

day

may

stay

play

away

boat

coat

toad

_____
bonus word

all
wall
call
will
tell
well
small
smell

_____
bonus word

cow
now
down
town
brown
show
row
low

_____
bonus word

car
far
jar
star
start
farm
harm
are

_____
bonus word

cut

cut

funny	saw	book
bunny	paw	good
puppy	law	look
penny	lawn	wood
happy	fawn	took
kitten	then	take
mitten	this	stood
little	what	stand

cut

cut

_____
bonus word

_____
bonus word

_____
bonus word

Spelling List

This Week's Focus:
- Spell short **a** words
- Recognize **a** as a special word

STEP **1** Trace and Spell	STEP **2** Copy and Spell	STEP **3** Cover and Spell

fold

1. an

2. at

3. and

4. am

5. a

6. _____
   bonus word

_____ _____

_____ _____

_____ _____

_____ _____

_____ _____

_____ _____

Fill in the boxes.

an   at   and   am   a

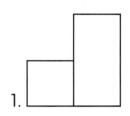

1.

2.

3.

4.

5.

Find the Mistakes

Mark an **X** on the misspelled words.

1. John ~~am~~ Mary are having fun.

2. That is an fox.

3. That is a ox.

4. Look ate that cat.

Write the missing word on the line.

1. I _____ sad.
   an, am

2. Don _____ Dan ran fast.
   an, and

3. She sat _____ the table.
   at, a

4. He has _____ cat.
   an, a

5. I ate _____ apple.
   a, an

My Spelling Dictation

Write the sentence.
Circle the spelling words.

_____

_____

_____

_____

22

Word Study

Fill in the missing letter.

1. _____ cat sat in a hat.

2. That is _____n oak tree.

3. I have a cat _____nd a dog.

4. I _____m six years old.

5. Look _____t that rat!

Rhyming Words

Match the words that rhyme.

an   cat

at   pan

and   Pam

am   sand

Spelling List

This Week's Focus:
- Spell short **i** words

STEP 1 Trace and Spell	STEP 2 Copy and Spell	STEP 3 Cover and Spell

fold

1. in

2. is

3. it

4. big

5. did

6. _____
   bonus word

Visual Memory

Fill in the boxes.

in   is   it   big   did

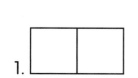

1.

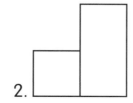

2.

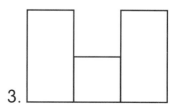

3.

4.

5.

Find the Correct Word

Circle the word that is spelled correctly.

1. ni   in

2. is   si

3. it   ti

4. gib   big

5. idd   did

25   Building Spelling Skills, Daily Practice • EMC 2705

Word Meaning

Fill in the missing word.

> in   is   it   big   did

1. What _____ she say?

2. Put your toys _____ the box.

3. That _____ a fun game.

4. I have a _____ dog.

5. Is _____ the color blue?

My Spelling Dictation

Write the sentence.
Circle the spelling words.

_____

_____

_____

_____

Word Study

Fill in the missing letter.

1. D____d you have fun?

2. Is that b____g?

3. Is ____t big?

4. ____s it ____n the box?

Find the Hidden Words

Make a circle around each spelling word.

in   is   it   big   did

1. i n i s i t b i g d i d

2. d i d b i g i t i s i n

3. i t i s d i d i n b i g

STEP 1 Trace and Spell	STEP 2 Copy and Spell	STEP 3 Cover and Spell

fold

1. can

2. pan

3. man

4. cat

5. sat

6. _____
   bonus word

Fill in the boxes.

can pan man cat sat

1.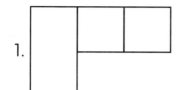

2.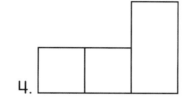

3.

4.

5.

Spell Correctly

Unscramble the letters.
Write the spelling words.

can pan man cat sat

anp _____

anm _____

anc _____

tac _____

tas _____

Word Meaning

Write the missing word on the line.

1. The _____ drove the bus.
   pan, man

2. I _____ tie my own shoes.
   can, pan

3. I _____ by my best friend.
   cat, sat

4. Stan has a cooking _____.
   sat, pan

5. My pet _____ is fat.
   sat, cat

My Spelling Dictation

Write the sentence.
Circle the spelling words.

_____

_____

_____

_____

Word Study

Read the words.
Write the words that rhyme in the correct box.

cat	pan	man	sat
can	pat	mat	tan

ran	rat
pan _____	_____ _____
_____ _____	_____ _____
_____ _____	_____ _____
_____ _____	_____ _____

Complete each rhyming word.

1. I gave a <u>pat</u>

   to my pet c_at____.

2. A fat <u>rat</u>

   sat on a m_____.

3. I see a <u>man</u>

   with a hot p_____.

4. My good friend <u>Dan</u>

   picks up a c_____.

Spelling List

This Week's Focus:
- Review short **a** and **i** words
- Review the -**an** word family

STEP 1 Trace and Spell

STEP 2 Copy and Spell

STEP 3 Cover and Spell

1. as
2. had
3. sit
4. six
5. ran
6. _____
   bonus word

fold

Visual Memory

Fill in the boxes.

as   had   sit   six   ran

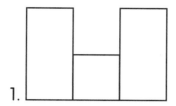

1.

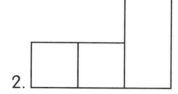

2.

3.

4.

5.

Find the Mistakes

Mark an **X** on the misspelled words.

1. ~~os~~   as

2. ran   rin

3. had   hed

4. sut   sit

5. six   cix

Fill in the missing word.

> as   had   sit   six   ran

1. My cat likes to _____ in that chair.

2. I have _____ cats.

3. I _____ five dogs.

4. Dogs are not _____ good as cats.

5. All my dogs _____ away.

My Spelling Dictation

Write the sentence.
Circle the spelling words.

_____

_____

_____

_____

Word Study

Write the letters **an** to make new words.

b_an_____   p_____

f_____   m_____

r_____   t_____

c_____   v_____

D_____

Find What's Missing

Fill in the missing letter.

as   had   sit   six   ran

s____t   r____n

ha____   a____

s____x   ____it

ra____   h____d

Spelling List

This Week's Focus:
- Spell short **u** words
- Recognize **to** as a special word

STEP 1 Trace and Spell	STEP 2 Copy and Spell	STEP 3 Cover and Spell

fold

1. up

2. us

3. run

4. fun

5. to

6. _____
   bonus word

Fill in the boxes.

up   us   run   fun   to

1.

2.

3.

4.

5.

Rhyming Words

Match the words that rhyme.

up	pup
us	fun
run	bus
to	do

Word Meaning

Write the missing word on the line.

1. I like _____ eat candy.
   us, to

2. Are you having _____?
   fun, run

3. Look _____ at the sky.
   us, up

4. Do not let the water _____ so long.
   to, run

5. Will you play with _____?
   to, us

My Spelling Dictation

Write the sentence.
Circle the spelling words.

_____

_____

_____

_____

Find the Hidden Words

Draw a circle around each spelling word.

> up   us   run   fun   to

1. t o r u n u p u s f u n

2. f u n r u n t o u p u s

3. t o u s f u n u p r u n

Find the Correct Word

Circle the words that are spelled correctly.

1. fun   fwn

2. yp   up

3. rwn   run

4. us   ys

5. to   tw

Spelling List

This Week's Focus:
- Spell short **u** words
- Recognize **I** as a special word

STEP 1 Trace and Spell

STEP 2 Copy and Spell

STEP 3 Cover and Spell

fold

1. pup

2. bus

3. but

4. tub

5. I

6. _____
   bonus word

Visual Memory

Fill in the boxes.

> pup   bus   but   tub   I

1.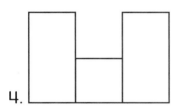

2.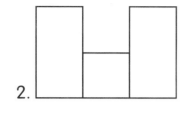

3.

4.

5.

Spell Correctly

Unscramble the letters.
Write the spelling words.

> pup   bus   but   tub

ppu _____   bsu _____

btu _____   tbu _____

upp _____   ubs _____

Word Meaning

Fill in the missing word.

> pup   bus   but   tub   I

1. Give the food to the _____.

2. The _____ stops here.

3. Wash up in the _____.

4. _____ want to play.

5. I like red, _____ not blue.

My Spelling Dictation

Write the sentence.
Circle the spelling words.

_____

_____

_____

_____

Word Study

Read the words. Listen for the short vowel sounds.
Write each word in the correct box.

pup	can	run	pan
man	tub	but	had
cat	sat	us	fun

up	and
pup _____	_____ _____
_____ _____	_____ _____
_____ _____	_____ _____
_____ _____	_____ _____

Change one letter to make a new word.

1. cup

   _p_ up

2. rub

   ____ub

3. Gus

   ____us

4. cut

   ____ut

Spelling List

This Week's Focus:
- Review short **i**, **a**, and **u** words
- Recognize the special vowel sound in **put**

STEP 1 Trace and Spell   **STEP 2 Copy and Spell**   **STEP 3 Cover and Spell**

fold

1. his
2. dig
3. pat
4. sun
5. put
6. _____
   bonus word

_____   _____

_____   _____

_____   _____

_____   _____

_____   _____

_____   _____

Visual Memory

Fill in the boxes.

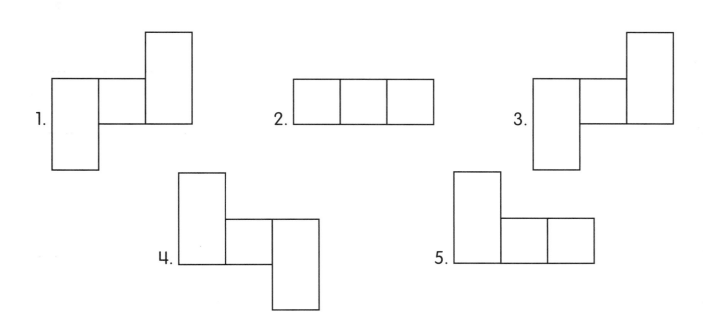

his   dig   pat   sun   put

1.

2.

3.

4.

5.

Find the Mistakes

Mark an **X** on the misspelled word in each sentence.
Write the words correctly on the lines.

1. That is ~~hes~~ book. _____his_____

2. I can dug a hole. _____

3. Please putt the book down. _____

4. The syn is hot. _____

5. You may pt the cat. _____

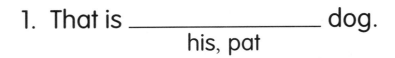

Write the missing word on the line.

1. That is _____ dog.
   his, pat

2. The _____ is hot today.
   his, sun

3. I like to _____ the dog.
   pat, put

4. Did you _____ that hole?
   put, dig

5. Please _____ the ball away.
   pat, put

My Spelling Dictation

Write the sentence.
Circle the spelling words.

_____

_____

_____

_____

Word Study

Read the words. Listen for the short vowel sounds.
Write each word in the correct box.

dig	sun	pat	his	but
sit	and	bus	run	cat
man	it			

as	**is**	**up**
cat	_____	_____
_____	_____	_____
_____	_____	_____
_____	_____	_____

Complete each rhyming word.

1. Will you <u>pat</u>

   my little c_____?

2. The fat <u>pig</u>

   loves to d_____.

3. We have <u>fun</u>

   in the s_____.

4. That <u>is</u>

   not h_____.

47

Spelling List

This Week's Focus:
- Spell short **o** words
- Recognize **the** as a special word

STEP 1 Trace and Spell	STEP 2 Copy and Spell	STEP 3 Cover and Spell

1. not
2. on
3. dog
4. got
5. the
6. _____
   bonus word

fold

Fill in the boxes.

not   on   dog   got   the

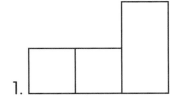

1.

2.

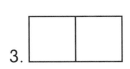

3.

4.

5.

Find the Mistakes

Mark an **X** on the misspelled word in each sentence.
Write the word correctly on the line.

1. I like to run with my dug. _____

2. Tha cat is playing. _____

3. Please get no the bus. _____

4. I gat a ball. _____

5. That is nat my cat. _____

Fill in the missing word.

> not   on   dog   got   the

1. A cat sat on _____ hat.

2. Do _____ play with the dog.

3. My pet is a _____.

4. I _____ a puppy.

5. The cat sleeps _____ my bed.

My Spelling Dictation

Write the sentence.
Circle the spelling words.

_____

_____

_____

_____

Find the Hidden Words

Draw a circle around each spelling word.

not   on   dog   got   the

1. t h e n o t o n d o g g o t

2. n o t o n d o g t h e g o t

3. n o t t h e g o t d o g o n

Find the Correct Word

Circle the words that are spelled correctly.

1. onn   on

2. tha   the

3. dog   dwg

4. got   gat

5. nawt   not

Spelling List

This Week's Focus:
- Spell short **e** words
- Spell words in the **-et** word family

STEP 1 Trace and Spell	STEP 2 Copy and Spell	STEP 3 Cover and Spell

fold

1. pet

2. get

3. let

4. fed

5. red

6. _____
   bonus word

_____   _____

_____   _____

_____   _____

_____   _____

_____   _____

_____   _____

Fill in the boxes.

pet   fed   let   get   red

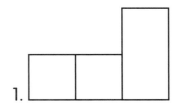

1.   2.

3.   4.   5.

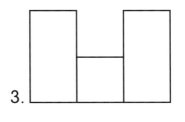 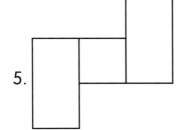

Spell Correctly

Unscramble the letters.
Write the spelling words.

pet   fed   let   get   red

def _____   tel _____

teg _____   der _____

tep _____   etp _____

Word Meaning

Write the missing word on the line.

1. The dog is the color _____ .

   pet, red

2. Please _____ me have a cat.

   let, pet

3. You may _____ my dog.

   let, pet

4. I _____ my pet.

   fed, red

5. I will _____ my cat.

   get, fed

My Spelling Dictation

Write the sentence.
Circle the spelling words.

_____

_____

_____

_____

Word Study

Add letters to make new words.

g   j   l   m   n   p   s   w

____g_et   _____et

_____et   _____et

_____et   _____et

_____et   _____et

Find the Correct Word

Circle the words that are spelled correctly.

1. fet   pet

2. fed   ped

3. ged   red

4. get   git

5. let   det

Spelling List

This Week's Focus:
- Review short **o**, **i**, and **e** words
- Recognize the **-op** and **-en** word families

STEP 1 Trace and Spell	STEP 2 Copy and Spell	STEP 3 Cover and Spell

fold

1. top
2. stop
3. men
4. fix
5. fox
6. _____
   bonus word

_____   _____

_____   _____

_____   _____

_____   _____

_____   _____

_____   _____

Fill in the boxes.

top   stop   men   fix   fox

1.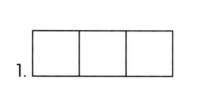

2.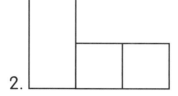

3.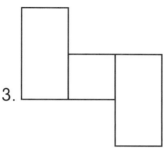

4.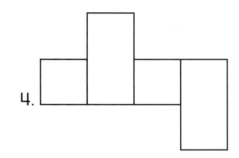

5.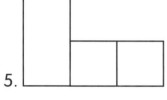

Find the Mistakes

Circle the misspelled word in each sentence.
Write the word correctly on the line.

1. Please stap the car. _____

2. The man are running fast. _____

3. Can you fex your toy? _____

4. The foxs is in a box. _____

5. The fox is on tap of the box. _____

Word Meaning

Write the missing word on the line.

1. The _____ got on the bus.
   fix, men

2. Please _____ the toy.
   fox, fix

3. Do not _____ running!
   stop, top

4. Did you see the _____?
   fix, fox

5. Put the toy on _____ of the box.
   stop, top

My Spelling Dictation

Write the sentence.
Circle the spelling words.

_____

_____

_____

_____

Word Study

Use the letters to make new words.

h   m   p   t

_____op   _____op   _____op   _____op

B   d   h   m   p   t

_____en   _____en   _____en

_____en   _____en   _____en

Find the Hidden Words

Draw a circle around each spelling word.

top   stop   men   fix   fox

1. m e n f i x f o x s t o p t o p

2. s t o p t o p f i x f o x m e n

3. f o x s t o p t o p f i x m e n

Spelling List

This Week's Focus:
- Review short **e**, **a**, and **o** words
- Practice with rhyming words

STEP 1 Trace and Spell	STEP 2 Copy and Spell	STEP 3 Cover and Spell

fold

1. ten
2. hat
3. hot
4. sand
5. hand
6. _____
   bonus word

Visual Memory

Fill in the boxes.

ten   hat   hot   sand   hand

1.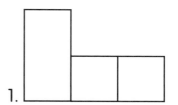

2.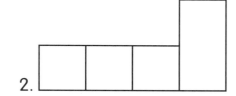

3.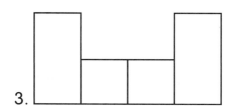

4.

5.

Find the Mistakes

Mark an **X** on the misspelled words.

1. sond   sand

2. hand   hond

3. hot   het

4. hat   hyt

5. tenn   ten

Fill in the missing word.

ten hat hot sand hand

1. He put a _____ on his head.

2. The water was _____.

3. She had a dime in her _____.

4. She had _____ pennies in her pocket.

5. He had _____ in his pail.

My Spelling Dictation

Write the sentence.
Circle the spelling words.

_____

_____

_____

_____

Word Study

Read the words. Listen for the short vowel sounds.
Write each word in the correct box.

hat	ten	and	hot
sat	not	pen	got
sand	at	hand	cat

hen	pat	pot	band
ten			

Complete each rhyming word.

1. I put my <u>hand</u>

   in the s_____.

2. A big red <u>hen</u>

   is in the p_____.

3. The big <u>pot</u>

   got too h_____.

4. A black <u>bat</u>

   has your h_____.

Spelling List

This Week's Focus:
• Spell plural forms of words

| STEP 1 Trace and Spell | STEP 2 Copy and Spell | STEP 3 Cover and Spell |

1. cats

2. pigs

3. beds

4. bugs

5. tops

6. _____
   bonus word

fold

Visual Memory

Fill in the boxes.

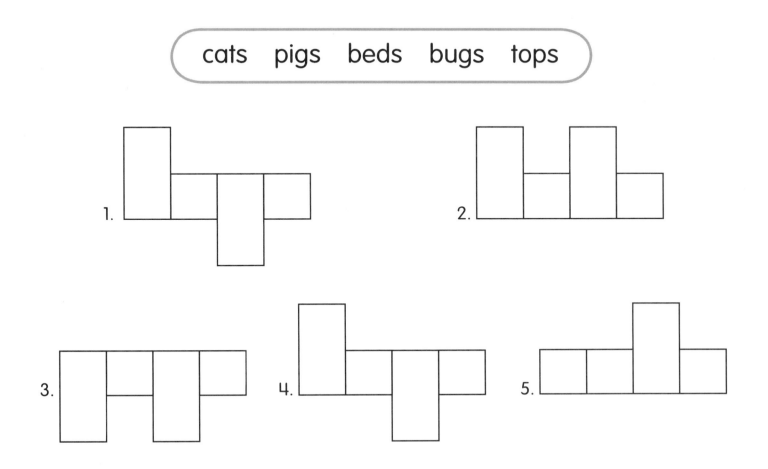

cats   pigs   beds   bugs   tops

1.

2.

3.

4.

5.

Using Plurals

Circle the correct sentence.

1. The cat was fed.

    The cats was fed.

2. The pigs were fed.

    The pig were fed.

3. The bed were made.

    The beds were made.

4. The bug was eating.

    The bugs was eating.

Word Meaning

Write the missing word on the line.

1. I have six _____.
   cat, cats

2. The _____ is in the pen.
   pig, pigs

3. Is your _____ made?
   bed, beds

4. There were ten _____ on the flower.
   bug, bugs

5. That is my _____.
   top, tops

My Spelling Dictation

Write the sentence.
Circle the spelling words.

_____

_____

_____

_____

Find the Correct Words

Circle the words that are spelled correctly.

tops	uss	pigs	hads	beds
feds	cats	thes	bugs	ons
pig	fixs	tops	nots	bug

Find the Hidden Words

Draw a circle around each spelling word.

cats   pigs   beds   bugs   tops

1. t o p s b e d s c a t s p i g s b u g s

2. t o p s b u g s c a t s b e d s p i g s

3. t o p s c a t s b u g s p i g s b e d s

Spelling List

This Week's Focus:
- Spell words that end with **ll**

STEP 1 Trace and Spell	STEP 2 Copy and Spell	STEP 3 Cover and Spell

fold

1. hill

2. bell

3. fell

4. ball

5. fall

6. _____
   bonus word

Visual Memory
Fill in the boxes.

hill   bell   fell   ball   fall

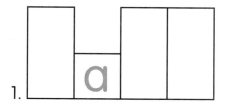

1.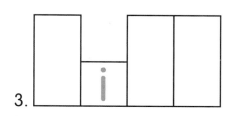

2.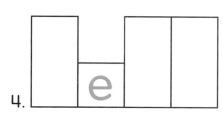

3.

4.

5.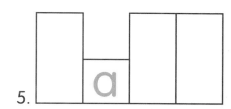

Spell Correctly

Unscramble the letters.
Write the spelling words.

lihl _____   lleb _____   flle _____

labl _____   allf _____   illh _____

elbl _____   elfl _____   albl _____

Fill in the missing word.

hill   bell   fell   ball   fall

1. Did you hear the _____ ring?

2. I went up the _____.

3. Yesterday I _____ down the hill.

4. I do not like to _____ down the hill.

5. Please kick the _____ to me.

My Spelling Dictation

Write the sentence.
Circle the spelling words.

_____

_____

_____

_____

Write a vowel in the space to make a spelling word.

a   e   i

b____ll   b____ll   h____ll

f____ll   f____ll

Word Meaning

Write the missing words on the lines.

fell   ball   fall   hill   bell

1. The _____ rolled down the _____.

2. I will _____ if you push me.

3. The _____ _____ out of my hand.

Spelling List

This Week's Focus:
- Spell words with the initial or final consonant digraph **sh**
- Recognize rhyming words

STEP 1 Trace and Spell

STEP 2 Copy and Spell

STEP 3 Cover and Spell

fold

1. she
2. ship
3. shell
4. dish
5. wish
6. _____
   bonus word

Visual Memory

Fill in the boxes.

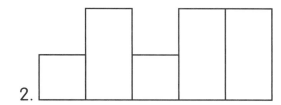

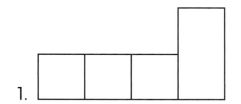

1.

2.

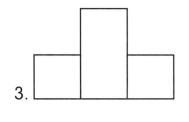

3.

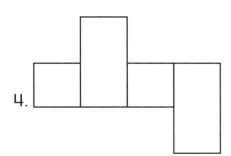

4.

5.

Find the Hidden Words

Draw a circle around each spelling word.

s h i p s h	s h w i s h	s h e s h
s h e l l s h	s h d i s h	s h s h i p
s h s h e	w i s h s h	s h s h e l l

Write the missing word on the line.

1. Put the _____ on the table.
   ship, dish

2. This _____ is from the ocean.
   she, shell

3. _____ was going to the store.
   She, Ship

4. I _____ for a pet dog.
   wish, ship

5. Were you on that _____?
   dish, ship

My Spelling Dictation

Write the sentence.
Circle the spelling words.

_____

_____

_____

_____

Word Meaning

Add a letter to make a new word.

b	c	d	f	s	w

ship   ____ip   ____ip

dish   ____ish   ____ish

shell   ____ell   ____ell   ____ell

Rhyming Words

Write the spelling words that rhyme.

she	ship	shell	dish	wish

1. fish   _____   _____

2. dip   _____

3. bell   _____

4. he   _____

        Building Spelling Skills, Daily Practice • EMC 2705

Spelling List

This Week's Focus:
- Spell long **a** words with silent **e**
- Recognize the short **u** sound in **come**

fold

1. make
2. came
3. lake
4. game
5. shake
6. ate
7. tape
8. come
9. _____
   bonus word

_____ _____

_____ _____

_____ _____

_____ _____

_____ _____

_____ _____

_____ _____

_____ _____

_____ _____

Visual Memory

Fill in the boxes.

make   came   lake   game   shake   ate   tape   come

1.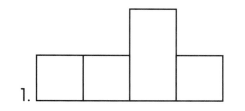

2.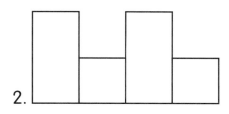

3.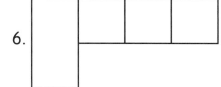

4.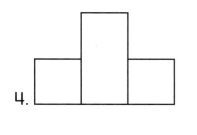

5.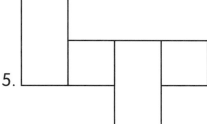

6.

7.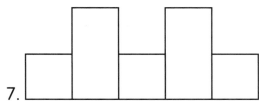

8.

Find the Mistakes

Mark an **X** on the misspelled words.

1. mak   make   5. came   kame

2. lake   lak   6. game   gaem

3. shake   shak   7. aet   ate

4. com   come   8. tayp   tape

Word Meaning

Write the missing words on the lines.

1. Please _____ my hand.
   shake, lake

2. I will _____ my art on the wall.
   tape, game

3. Will you _____ with me?
   come, came

4. I _____ the cake by the _____.
   tape, ate   lake, came

5. Did you _____ that _____?
   make, came   game, come

My Spelling Dictation

Write the sentence.
Circle the spelling words.

_____

_____

_____

_____

Word Study

Read the words. Listen for the vowel sounds.
Write each word in the correct box.

sand	make	had	came
game	hand	lake	shake
ran	ate	tape	pat

ate	hat
_____ _____	_____ _____
_____ _____	_____ _____
_____ _____	_____ _____
_____ _____	_____ _____

Change one letter to make a spelling word.

1. bake

   ____ake

2. same

   ____ame

3. cape

   ____ape

4. rake

   ____ake

This Week's Focus:
- Spell long **i** words with silent **e**
- Spell words with the long **i** sound spelled **y**

STEP 1 Trace and Spell   **STEP 2 Copy and Spell**   **STEP 3 Cover and Spell**

fold

1. five
2. time
3. like
4. dime
5. ride
6. nine
7. my
8. by
9. _____
   bonus word

_____   _____

_____   _____

_____   _____

_____   _____

_____   _____

_____   _____

_____   _____

_____   _____

_____   _____

five   time   like   dime   ride   nine   my   by

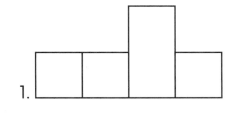

1.

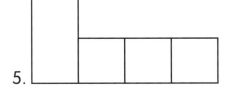

2.

3.

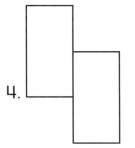

4.

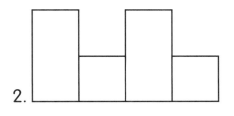

5.

6.

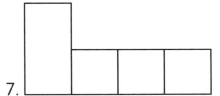

7.

8.

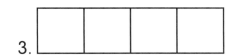

Find the Mistakes

Mark an **X** on the misspelled words.

1. five	fif	5. tyme	time
2. lik	like	6. dyme	dime
3. ride	ryde	7. nine	nyne
4. mi	my	8. bi	by

Word Meaning

Write the missing words on the lines.

1. One penny plus _____ pennies equals a _____.
   nine, like   time, dime

2. I need a _____ home.
   nine, ride

3. The _____ is _____ p.m.
   time, like   by, five

4. I _____ to run _____ the lake.
   like, dime   five, by

5. You may pet _____ dog.
   like, my

My Spelling Dictation

Write the sentences.
Circle the spelling words.

1. _____

   _____

2. _____

   _____

Word Study

Read the words. Listen for the vowel sounds.
Write each word in the correct box.

it	dime	pig	like
big	did	nine	five
ride	sit	six	dig
by	his	time	

dive	**is**
_____ _____	_____ _____
_____ _____	_____ _____
_____ _____	_____ _____
_____ _____	_____ _____

Change one letter to make a spelling word.

1. hive

____ive

2. bike

____ike

3. by

____y

4. side

____ide

5. time

____ime

6. mine

____ine

This Week's Focus:
• Review long **a** and **i** words with silent **e**

STEP 1 Trace and Spell

STEP 2 Copy and Spell

STEP 3 Cover and Spell

fold

1. gate

2. rake

3. name

4. bake

5. fine

6. bike

7. hide

8. mine

9. _____
   bonus word

Visual Memory

Fill in the boxes.

gate   rake   name   bake   fine   bike   hide   mine

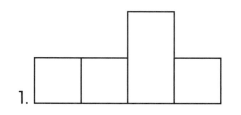

1.

2.

3.

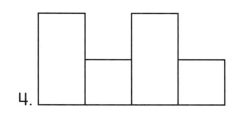

4.

5.

6.

7.

8.

Final Sounds

Add ending letters to make spelling words.

te   ke   me   ne   de

1. ra_____   3. ga_____   5. mi_____   7. na_____

2. fi_____   4. ba_____   6. bi_____   8. hi_____

       85

Word Meaning

Fill in the missing words.

> gate   rake   name   bake   fine   bike   hide   mine

1. I can ride my _____.

2. I _____ the leaves.

3. Please open the _____.

4. I like to _____ from my friends.

5. Please _____ a cake that is all _____.

6. My _____ is Ted, and that is _____ with me.

My Spelling Dictation

Write the sentences.
Circle the spelling words.

1. _____

   _____

2. _____

   _____

Word Study

Read the words. Listen for the vowel sounds.
Write each word in the correct box.

bake	can	name	pan
rake	gate	man	cat
sand	came	make	hand
lake	pat	hat	game

rate	as
_____ _____	_____ _____
_____ _____	_____ _____
_____ _____	_____ _____
_____ _____	_____ _____

Complete each rhyming word.

1. I meet <u>Kate</u>

   at the g_____.

2. We <u>dine</u>

   at n_____.

3. Will you <u>take</u>

   the red r_____?

4. Do you <u>like</u>

   your new b_____?

87

Spelling List

This Week's Focus:
- Spell words with the long **e** sound spelled **e** and **ee**

| STEP 1 Trace and Spell | STEP 2 Copy and Spell | STEP 3 Cover and Spell |

fold

1. we

2. me

3. he

4. be

5. see

6. need

7. tree

8. sheep

9. _____
bonus word

Fill in the boxes.

we   me   he   be

see   need   tree   sheep

1.

2.

3.

4.

5.

6.

7.

8.

Word Study

Fill in the blanks to make spelling words.
Use the words you made to complete the sentence.

e   ee

sh_____p   b_____   w_____   tr_____

s_____   h_____   m_____   n_____d

W_____ s_____ the sh_____p.

Write the missing words on the lines.

1. I will _____ careful up in the _____.
   be, he   we, tree

2. I _____ to feed the _____.
   need, we   sheep, be

3. Will you go with _____ to _____ that bee?
   me, be   see, tree

4. What will _____ do now?
   we, me

5. Did _____ get stung by the bee?
   be, he

My Spelling Dictation

Write the sentences.
Circle the spelling words.

1. _____

   _____

2. _____

   _____

Word Study

Read the words. Listen for the vowel sounds.
Write each word in the correct box.

fed	we	me	red
he	be	tree	see
ten	get	let	men
need	free	bed	

be	**pet**
_____ _____	_____ _____
_____ _____	_____ _____
_____ _____	_____ _____
_____ _____	_____ _____

Complete each rhyming word.

1. Who will <u>be</u>

   there with m_____?

2. This is the <u>seed</u>

   that I will n_____.

3. Can you <u>see</u>

   that big t_____?

4. I can <u>keep</u>

   the white s_____.

Spelling List

This Week's Focus:
• Spell words with the long **o** sound
• Recognize **do** and **you** as special words

STEP 1 Trace and Spell   **STEP 2 Copy and Spell**   **STEP 3 Cover and Spell**

fold

1. go

2. so

3. no

4. home

5. note

6. robe

7. do

8. you

9. _____
bonus word

Visual Memory

Fill in the boxes.

go so no home note robe do you

1.

2.

3.

4.

5.

6.

7.

8.

Find the Correct Word

Circle the words that are spelled correctly.

1. yow   (you)   euw

2. do   duw   doo

3. roob   roub   robe

4. noot   note   nowt

5. home   howm   hom

6. nw   noo   no

7. sw   su   so

8. go   gw   gow

Word Meaning

Write the missing words on the lines.

1. What game _____ you want to play?
   no, do

2. I want to _____ _____.
   go, note   robe, home

3. Did _____ write a _____?
   home, you   so, note

4. I wear a _____ in the morning.
   do, robe

5. I stopped running _____ you could catch up.
   go, so

My Spelling Dictation

Write the sentences.
Circle the spelling words.

1. _____

   _____

2. _____

   _____

Word Study

Read the words. Listen for the vowel sounds.
Write each word in the correct box.

not	dog	go	so
hop	home	on	top
note	fox	robe	stop
mop	row		

no	hot
_____ _____	_____ _____
_____ _____	_____ _____
_____ _____	_____ _____
_____ _____	_____ _____

Change one letter to make a spelling word.

1. no

    ____o

2. vote

    ____ote

3. dome

    ____ome

4. lobe

    ____obe

Spelling List

This Week's Focus:
- Review words with long vowel sounds made with a silent **e**
- Review words with the long **e** sound spelled **ee**

STEP 1 Trace and Spell	STEP 2 Copy and Spell	STEP 3 Cover and Spell

fold

1. late

2. gave

3. cone

4. line

5. snake

6. feet

7. jeep

8. use

9. _____
   bonus word

Fill in the boxes.

> | late | feet | cone | line |
> | snake | gave | jeep | use |

1.

2.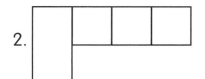

3.

4.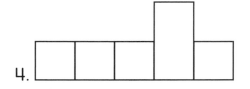

5.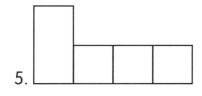

6.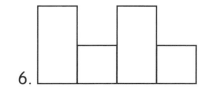

7.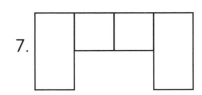

8.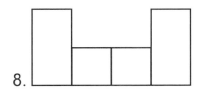

Find the Hidden Words

Draw a circle around each spelling word.

> late   feet   cone   line   snake   gave   jeep   use

1. snakegavejeepuselineconefeetlate

2. snakejeepuselineconefeetlategave

3. usejeepgavesnakelinefeetconelate

Word Meaning

Circle the answers.

1. What holds ice cream?   line   cone   snake

2. Which one is an animal?   snake   cone   jeep

3. What do you stand on?   jeep   feet   snake

4. What can you ride in?   feet   line   jeep

5. What do you stand in?   line   cone   snake

My Spelling Dictation

Write the sentences.
Circle the spelling words.

1. _____

_____

2. _____

_____

Word Study

Read the words. Listen for the long vowel sounds.
Write each word in the correct box.

go	fine	jeep	late
shake	need	bye	cone
be	by	bee	lake
gave	me	nine	home

long **a**	long **e**	long **i**	long **o**
_____	_____	_____	_____
_____	_____	_____	_____
_____	_____	_____	_____
_____	_____	_____	_____
_____	_____	_____	_____

Complete each rhyming word.

1. I will <u>take</u>

   my pet s_____.

2. You can <u>keep</u>

   my toy j_____.

3. I have a <u>phone</u>

   and an ice-cream c_____.

4. I see <u>nine</u>

   in the l_____.

STEP 1 Trace and Spell | **STEP 2** Copy and Spell | **STEP 3** Cover and Spell

fold

1. ropes
2. bones
3. kites
4. bees
5. cakes
6. boxes
7. foxes
8. roses
9. _____
   bonus word

Visual Memory

Fill in the boxes.

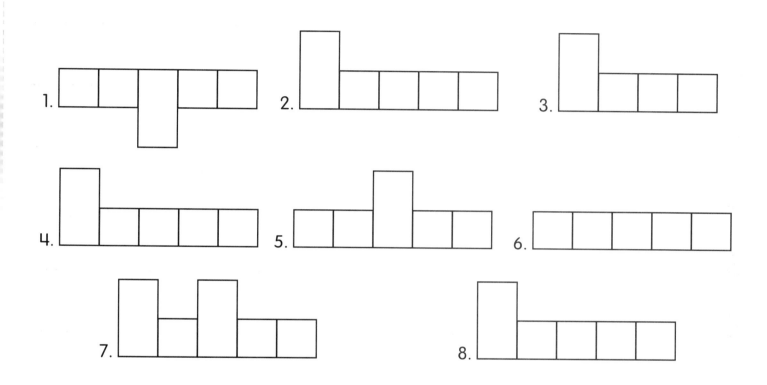

| ropes | bones | kites | bees |
| cakes | boxes | foxes | roses |

Find the Hidden Words

Draw a circle around each spelling word.

1. b o n e s b o x e s f o x e s r o s e s k i t e s c a k e s

2. r o s e s b e e s b o n e s f o x e s b o x e s r o s e s

3. b o n e s r o p e s c a k e s r o s e s b e e s f o x e s

101

Word Meaning

Write the missing word on the line.

1. My dad made two _____.
   cakes, cake

2. I can climb a _____.
   ropes, rope

3. How many _____ do you need?
   boxes, box

4. I can fly a _____.
   kites, kite

5. Here are ten _____.
   roses, rose

6. Did you see that _____?
   foxes, fox

My Spelling Dictation

Write the sentences.
Circle the spelling words.

1. _____

   _____

2. _____

   _____

Word Study

Add **s** or **es** to make a new word.

1. bee_____

2. rose_____

3. bone_____

4. cake_____

5. box_____

6. kite_____

7. fox_____

8. rope_____

9. fix_____

10. lake_____

11. note_____

12. mix_____

13. tree_____

14. make_____

Find the Mistakes

Mark an **X** on the misspelled words.

1. foxs   foxes

2. boxs   boxes

3. bones   bonees

4. beees   bees

5. kites   kitees

Spelling List

This Week's Focus:
• Spell words that end in **nt** and **nd**

fold

1. went
2. sent
3. ant
4. bend
5. find
6. mind
7. kind
8. want
9. _____
   bonus word

Visual Memory

Fill in the boxes.

> went   sent   ant   bend
>
> find   mind   kind   want

1.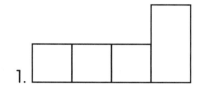

2.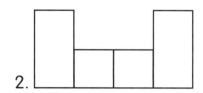

3.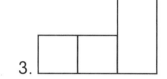

4.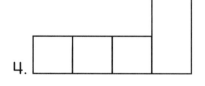

5.

6.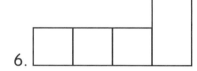

7.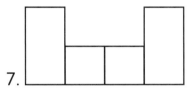

8.

Spell Vowel Sounds

Fill in the missing vowel to make a word. Write **a**, **e**, or **i**.

1. w___nt

2. w___nt

3. b___nd

4. b___nd

5. b___nd

6. f___nd

7. m___nd

8. m___nd

9. k___nd

       Building Spelling Skills, Daily Practice • EMC 2705

Word Meaning

Fill in the missing word.

> went   sent   ant   bend   find   mind   kind   want

1. I _____ you some flowers.

2. You should always be _____ to animals.

3. Please _____ a seat.

4. Was there an _____ in your food?

5. I _____ to school.

6. I use my _____ at school.

My Spelling Dictation

Write the sentences.
Circle the spelling words.

1. _____

   _____

2. _____

   _____

Word Study

Add **nt** or **nd** to make a word.

1. fi_nd_____   7. mi_____

2. wa_____   8. mi_____

3. wa_____   9. a_____

4. we_____   10. a_____

5. se_____   11. be_____

6. se_____   12. be_____

Find the Mistakes

Mark an **X** on the misspelled word in each sentence.
Write the word correctly on the line.

1. She wint to the store.   _____

2. He sint me a card.   _____

3. I cannot fined my dog.   _____

4. Did you see the ante?   _____

5. There is a beend in the road.   _____

6. Use your mynd to think.   _____

Spelling List

This Week's Focus:
- Spell words with initial or final **st**

STEP 1 Trace and Spell

STEP 2 Copy and Spell

STEP 3 Cover and Spell

fold

1. fast
2. last
3. nest
4. must
5. most
6. step
7. stamp
8. still
9. _____
   bonus word

Visual Memory

Fill in the boxes.

> fast   last   nest   must
>
> most   step   stamp   still

1.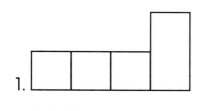

2.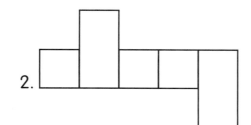

3.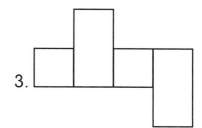

4.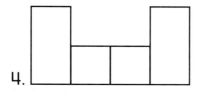

5.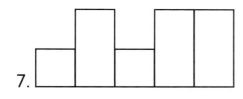

6.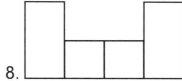

7.

8.

Spell Correctly

Unscramble the letters. Write the spelling words.

> fast   last   nest   must   most   step   stamp   still

epts _____   omts _____

ents _____   alts _____

itlsl _____   apmts _____

umts _____   afts _____

Word Meaning

Fill in the missing word.

| fast last nest must most step stamp still |

1. Did you _____ on the cat's tail?

2. Who has the _____ pets?

3. Did you see the bird's _____?

4. Did you put a _____ on that letter?

5. Who can sit _____ the longest?

6. Who was first, and who was _____?

7. Who can run _____?

8. I _____ stop asking questions.

My Spelling Dictation

Write the sentences.
Circle the spelling words.

1. _____

_____

2. _____

_____

Word Study

Add **st** to make a spelling word.

ne_____   mo_____   _____ep   fa_____

_____amp   la_____   mu_____   _____ill

Use the words you made to fill in the blanks.

1. If you run _____, you will not be _____.

2. The bird _____ make a _____.

3. I am _____ being careful not to _____ on the cat.

Find the Hidden Words

Draw a circle around each spelling word.

nest   step   last   most   still   must   fast   stamp

1. n e s t s t a m p m u s t s t e p m o s t s t i l l f a s t l a s t

2. s t i l l f a s t s t a m p l a s t s t e p n e s t m o s t m u s t

3. s t i l l s t a m p s t e p m o s t m u s t n e s t l a s t f a s t

Spelling List

This Week's Focus:
- Spell words with the vowel digraphs **ay** and **oa**

STEP 1 Trace and Spell	STEP 2 Copy and Spell	STEP 3 Cover and Spell

fold

1. day
2. may
3. stay
4. play
5. away
6. boat
7. coat
8. toad
9. _____
   bonus word

Visual Memory

Fill in the boxes.

day   may   stay   play
away   boat   coat   toad

1.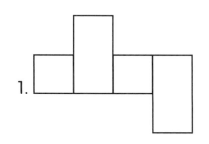

2.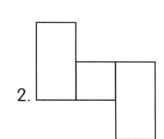

3.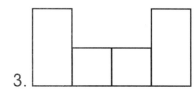

4.

5.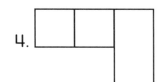

6.

7.

8.

Find the Mistakes

Mark an **X** on the misspelled words.

1. stae   stay

2. awy   away

3. may   mae

4. day   dae

5. plae   play

6. bot   boat

7. coat   koat

8. tood   toad

Word Meaning

Write the missing words on the lines.

1. What _____ do you want to _____?
   day, may   away, play

2. Will you _____ and not run _____?
   stay, day   away, may

3. What _____ I _____ with next?
   coat, may   boat, play

4. There is a _____ on the lake.
   boat, may

5. You _____ need a _____ in this rain.
   may, day   coat, away

6. I have a _____ as a pet.
   coat, toad

My Spelling Dictation

Write the sentences.
Circle the spelling words.

1. _____

   _____

2. _____

   _____

Word Study

Add letters to make words.

> aw cl gr pl st tr

_____ay   _____ay   _____ay

_____ay   _____ay   _____ay

Use the words you made to complete the sentences.

1. How long may I _____ to _____ this game?

2. Please put the _____ crayon _____ in the box.

Add a letter to make a word.

> b c g

_____oat   _____oat   _____oat

Use the words you made to complete the sentence.

You will need a _____ to ride in the _____.

Spelling List

This Week's Focus:
- Review words in the **-all**, **-ill**, and **-ell** word families

| STEP 1 Trace and Spell | STEP 2 Copy and Spell | STEP 3 Cover and Spell |

fold

1. all
2. wall
3. call
4. will
5. tell
6. well
7. small
8. smell
9. _____
   bonus word

Visual Memory

Fill in the boxes.

all	wall	call	will
tell	well	small	smell

1.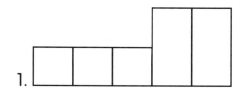

2.

3.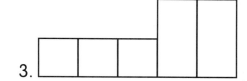

4.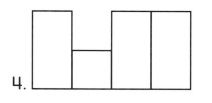

5.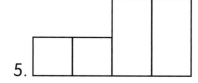

6.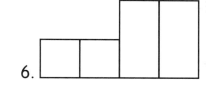

7.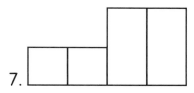

8.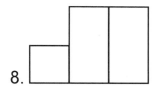

Find the Hidden Words

Draw a circle around each spelling word.

1. s m a l l a l l w a l l c a l l w i l l t e l l w e l l s m e l l

2. w a l l w i l l w e l l a l l c a l l t e l l s m a l l s m e l l

3. a l l c a l l w a l l s m a l l s m e l l w i l l t e l l w e l l

 Building Spelling Skills, Daily Practice • EMC 2705

Word Meaning

Fill in the missing word.

> all   wall   call   will   tell   well   small   smell

1. Can you _____ the flower?

2. You look sick. Are you feeling _____?

3. That is _____ I can do today.

4. The ball went over the _____.

5. May I _____ you on the phone?

6. I _____ pick up all my toys.

7. You have a large dog, and I have a _____ dog.

8. I want to _____ you a story.

My Spelling Dictation

Write the sentences.
Circle the spelling words.

1. _____

_____

2. _____

_____

Word Study

Add letters to make words.

$$\boxed{\text{all} \quad \text{ell} \quad \text{ill}}$$

w_____   b_____   t_____

w_____   b_____   f_____

w_____   b_____   f_____

sm_____   t_____   f_____

sm_____   t_____

Spell Vowel Sounds

Fill in the missing vowel. Write **a**, **e**, or **i**.

w____ll   w____ll   w____ll

s____ll   t____ll   t____ll

sm____ll   sm____ll   p____ll

Spelling List

This Week's Focus:
- Spell words with the vowel digraph **ow**

STEP 1 Trace and Spell	STEP 2 Copy and Spell	STEP 3 Cover and Spell

fold

1. cow
2. now
3. down
4. town
5. brown
6. show
7. row
8. low
9. _____
   bonus word

Visual Memory

Fill in the boxes.

> cow   now   down   town
>
> brown   show   row   low

1.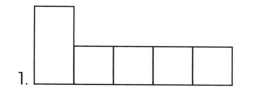

2.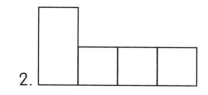

3.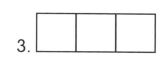

4.

5.

6.

7.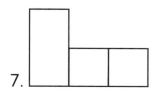

8.

Final Sounds

Add ending letters to make spelling words.
Use the words you made to complete the sentence.

> ow   own

c_____   sh_____   r_____   d_____

br_____   l_____   t_____   n_____

We are _____ walking _____ the stairs.

Building Spelling Skills, Daily Practice • EMC 2705

Write the missing words on the lines.

1. The _____ is the color _____.
   show, cow   brown, town

2. Can you _____ me the _____?
   show, now   down, town

3. What do you want to do _____?
   brown, now

4. Did you see that _____ of people sit _____?
   row, show   down, low

5. Would you _____ me how to _____ a boat?
   now, show   low, row

My Spelling Dictation

Write the sentences.
Circle the spelling words.

1. _____

   _____

2. _____

   _____

Word Study

Read the words. Listen for the sounds of **ow**.
Write each word in the correct box.

cow	now	row	brown
low	town	down	show
how	tow	blow	grow

pow	mow
COW _____	_____ _____
_____ _____	_____ _____
_____ _____	_____ _____
_____ _____	_____ _____

Complete each rhyming word.

1. How <u>now</u>,

   brown c_____?

2. I wear a <u>bow</u>

   to the new s_____.

3. We walk <u>down</u>

   to the t_____.

4. We seem <u>slow</u>

   when we r_____.

Spelling List

This Week's Focus:
- Spell words with **ar**

STEP 1 Trace and Spell

STEP 2 Copy and Spell

STEP 3 Cover and Spell

fold

1. car
2. far
3. jar
4. star
5. start
6. farm
7. harm
8. are
9. _____
   bonus word

Visual Memory

Fill in the boxes.

car   far   jar   star

start   farm   harm   are

1.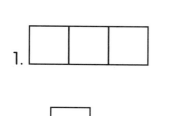

2.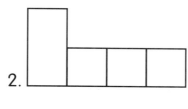

3.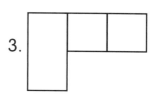

4.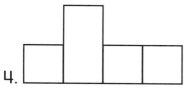

5.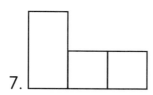

6.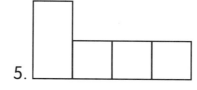

7.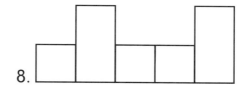

8.

Final Sounds

Add ending letters to make spelling words.
Use the words you made to complete the sentence.

ar   art   arm

c_____   f_____   f_____

h_____   j_____   st_____   st_____

The key would not _____ the _____.

Word Meaning

Fill in the missing words.

| car far jar star start farm harm are |

1. We drove the _____ to the _____.

2. Do you see the _____ in the sky?

3. Did you _____ to open that _____ of jam?

4. There is no _____ in walking on the grass.

5. What _____ your names?

My Spelling Dictation

Write the sentences.
Circle the spelling words.

1. _____

   _____

2. _____

   _____

Word Study

Read the words. Listen to the sounds of **a**.
Write the words in the correct boxes.

man	came	farm	sat
shake	star	pat	ate
car	and	tape	jar

are	can	make
_____	_____	_____
_____	_____	_____
_____	_____	_____
_____	_____	_____

Complete each rhyming word.

1. Is it <u>far</u>

   to the c_____?

2. Will any <u>harm</u>

   come to the f_____?

3. The go-<u>kart</u>

   will not s_____.

4. Put the candy <u>bar</u>

   in the open j_____.

Spelling List

This Week's Focus:
- Practice words with double consonants

STEP 1 Trace and Spell	STEP 2 Copy and Spell	STEP 3 Cover and Spell

fold

1. funny

2. bunny

3. puppy

4. penny

5. happy

6. kitten

7. mitten

8. little

9. _____
   bonus word

Visual Memory

Fill in the boxes.

> funny   bunny   puppy   penny
>
> happy   kitten   mitten   little

1.

2.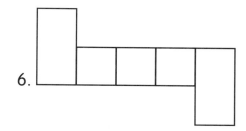

3.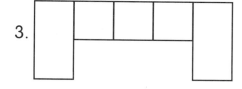

4.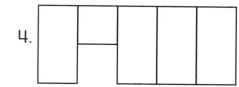

5.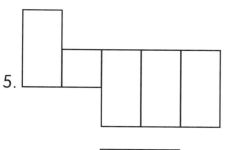

6.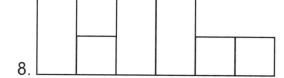

7.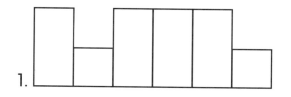

8.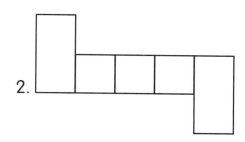

Find the Hidden Words

Draw a circle around each spelling word.

1. p e n n y p u p p y b u n n y f u n n y k i t t e n m i t t e n

2. p e n n y h a p p y p u p p y f u n n y k i t t e n l i t t l e

3. l i t t l e m i t t e n k i t t e n h a p p y b u n n y p e n n y

Write the missing word on the line.

1. The _____ was brown.
   funny, puppy

2. The _____ can run.
   funny, bunny

3. The kitten was _____.
   mitten, little

4. I can put a _____ in my hand.
   penny, little

5. I lost my _____ in the snow.
   mitten, little

My Spelling Dictation

Write the sentences.
Circle the spelling words.

1. _____

   _____

2. _____

   _____

Final Sounds

Add ending letters to make spelling words.
Use the words you made to complete the sentences.

> nny   ppy   tten

bu_____   mi_____   ha_____   pu_____

ki_____   fu_____   pe_____

1. A baby cat is called a _____.

2. A baby rabbit is called a _____.

3. A baby dog is called a _____.

Spell Correctly

Unscramble the letters.
Write the spelling words.

> funny   bunny   penny   happy   mitten   little

eynnp _____   ayhpp _____

eimntt _____   uyfnn _____

uybnn _____   tiltel _____

Spelling List

This Week's Focus:
- Spell words with the vowel digraph **aw**
- Spell words with the initial consonant digraph **th**
- Recognize **what** as a special word

STEP 1 Trace and Spell	STEP 2 Copy and Spell	STEP 3 Cover and Spell

fold

1. saw
2. paw
3. law
4. lawn
5. fawn
6. then
7. this
8. what
9. _____
   bonus word

Fill in the boxes.

| saw | paw | law | lawn |
| fawn | then | this | what |

1.

2.

3.

4.

5.

6.

7.

8.

Final Sounds

Add ending letters to make spelling words.
Use the words you made to complete the sentence.

l_____   l_____   s_____   p_____   f_____

I _____ a _____ walking in the woods.

Building Spelling Skills, Daily Practice • EMC 2705

Write the missing words on the lines.

1. Do you see the ＿＿＿＿＿＿＿＿ on the ＿＿＿＿＿＿＿＿?
   this, fawn   lawn, saw

2. I never break the ＿＿＿＿＿＿＿＿.
   law, paw

3. I ＿＿＿＿＿＿＿＿ the puppy's ＿＿＿＿＿＿＿＿.
   lawn, saw   fawn, paw

4. Do you know ＿＿＿＿＿＿＿＿ ＿＿＿＿＿＿＿＿ is?
   what, then   this, saw

5. Please wash your hands and ＿＿＿＿＿＿＿＿ come eat.
   this, then

My Spelling Dictation

Write the sentences.
Circle the spelling words.

1. ＿＿＿＿＿＿＿＿＿＿＿＿＿＿＿＿＿＿＿＿＿＿

   ＿＿＿＿＿＿＿＿＿＿＿＿＿＿＿＿＿＿＿＿＿＿

2. ＿＿＿＿＿＿＿＿＿＿＿＿＿＿＿＿＿＿＿＿＿＿

   ＿＿＿＿＿＿＿＿＿＿＿＿＿＿＿＿＿＿＿＿＿＿

Write the words that rhyme.

> brown   fawn   now   law   row   men   saw

1. then _____

2. lawn _____

3. paw _____

4. town _____

5. jaw _____

6. cow _____

7. show _____

Spell Correctly

Unscramble the letters.
Write the spelling words.

> saw   paw   law   lawn   fawn   then   this   what

wafn _____

wath _____

wal _____

pwa _____

nawl _____

enth _____

aws _____

tsih _____

Spelling List

This Week's Focus:
- Spell words with the vowel sound in **book**
- Practice present and past tense words
- Spell words in the **-ook, -ood,** and **-and** word families

STEP 1 Trace and Spell   **STEP 2 Copy and Spell**   **STEP 3 Cover and Spell**

fold

1. book
2. good
3. look
4. wood
5. took
6. take
7. stood
8. stand
9. _____
   bonus word

Visual Memory

Fill in the boxes.

> book   good   look   wood
>
> took   take   stood   stand

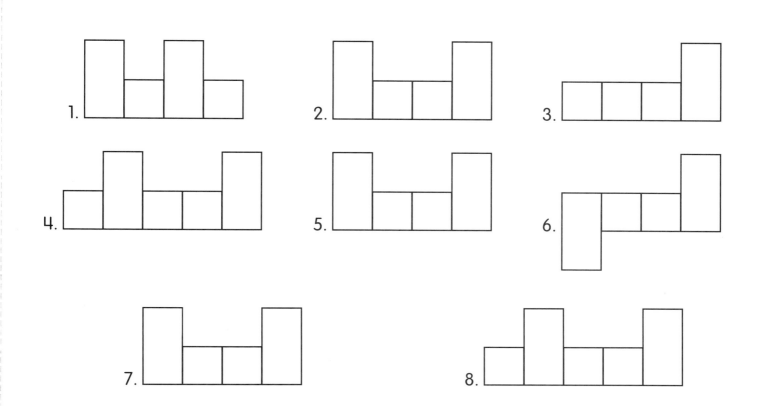

Find the Hidden Words

Draw a circle around each spelling word.

1. b o o k g o o d l o o k w o o d t o o k s t o o d t a k e

2. w o o d t a k e s t o o d s t a n d l o o k g o o d b o o k

3. t o o k s t a n d s t o o d t a k e w o o d b o o k l o o k

4. b o o k l o o k t o o k g o o d w o o d s t o o d s t a n d

137

Word Meaning

Write the missing words on the lines.

1. Do you want to _____ at this _____?
   take, look   took, book

2. Do you want to _____ the puppy home?
   take, took

3. I _____ the puppy home.
   take, took

4. May I _____ next to you?
   stood, stand

5. I _____ next to you this morning.
   stood, stand

6. I like to make things from _____.
   wood, took

My Spelling Dictation

Write the sentences.
Circle the spelling words.

1. _____

   _____

2. _____

   _____

Final Sounds

Add ending letters to make words.
Use the words you made to complete the sentences.

ook   ood

l_____   b_____   g_____   t_____

st_____   w_____   f_____   c_____

1. I _____ at the store window to _____ at the toys.

2. I like to eat _____ when I read a _____.

Add ending letters to make words.
Use the words you made to complete the sentences.

and

st_____   b_____   h_____   l_____

s_____   gr_____   gl_____   bl_____

1. Please _____ when the _____ plays.

2. The white _____ is _____.

Spelling Record Sheet

Building Spelling Skills

Students' Names															
1															
2															
3															
4															
5															
6															
7															
8															
9															
10															
11															
12															
13															
14															
15															
16															
17															
18															
19															
20															
21															
22															
23															
24															
25															
26															
27															
28															
29															
30															

Note: Reproduce this form twice for each student to track his or her progress.

My Spelling Record

Spelling List	Date	Number Correct	Words Missed

My Spelling Test

Listen to the words.
Write each word on a line.

1. _____

2. _____

3. _____

4. _____

5. _____

6. _____

7. _____

8. _____

9. _____

Good luck!

My Spelling Dictation

Listen to the sentences.
Write them on the lines.

1. _____

_____

2. _____

_____

Building Spelling Skills

Spelling List

STEP 1 Trace and Spell

STEP 2 Copy and Spell

STEP 3 Cover and Spell

fold

1. _____

2. _____

3. _____

4. _____

5. _____

6. _____

7. _____

8. _____

9. _____

Building Spelling Skills

Word Box

Building Spelling Skills

Dear Parents,

Attached is your child's spelling list for this week. Encourage him or her to practice the words in one or more of these ways:

1. Read and spell each word. Cover it up and write it. Uncover the word and check to see if it is correct.
2. Find the words on the spelling list in printed materials such as books and magazines.
3. Read a word aloud and ask your child to spell it (either aloud or written on paper).

Thank you for your support of our spelling program.

Sincerely,

Building Spelling Skills

Dear Parents,

Attached is your child's spelling list for this week. Encourage him or her to practice the words in one or more of these ways:

1. Read and spell each word. Cover it up and write it. Uncover the word and check to see if it is correct.
2. Find the words on the spelling list in printed materials such as books and magazines.
3. Read a word aloud and ask your child to spell it (either aloud or written on paper).

Thank you for your support of our spelling program.

Sincerely,

Student Spelling Dictionaries

Self-made spelling dictionaries provide students with a reference for words they frequently use in their writing.

Materials

- copy of "My Own Spelling Dictionary" form (page 147)
- 26 sheets of lined paper—6" x 9" (15 x 23 cm)
- 2 sheets of construction paper or tagboard for cover—6" x 9" (15 x 23 cm)
- crayons or markers
- glue
- stapler
- masking tape

Steps to Follow

1 Color and cut out the cover sheet form. Glue it to the front cover of the dictionary.

2 Staple the lined paper inside the cover. Place masking tape over the staples.

3 Guide students (or ask parent volunteers) to write a letter of the alphabet on each page.

What to Include

1. When students ask for the correct spelling of a special word, have them write it in their dictionary.

2. Include special words being learned as part of science or social studies units.

3. Include words for special holidays.

4. Include the common words students continue to misspell on tests and in daily written work.

5. Add color and number words if these are not on charts posted in the classroom.

—— My Own ——
Spelling Dictionary

Name _____

—— My Own ——
Spelling Dictionary

Name _____

Master Word List

a	bugs	far	harm
all	bunny	farm	hat
am	bus	fast	he
an	but	fawn	hide
and	by	fed	hill
ant	cakes	feet	his
are	call	fell	home
as	came	find	hot
at	can	fine	I
ate	car	five	in
away	cat	fix	is
bake	cats	fox	it
ball	coat	foxes	jar
be	come	fun	jeep
beds	cone	funny	kind
bees	cow	game	kites
bell	day	gate	kitten
bend	did	gave	lake
big	dig	get	last
bike	dime	go	late
boat	dish	good	law
bones	do	got	lawn
book	dog	had	let
boxes	down	hand	like
brown	fall	happy	line

little	paw	shell	this
look	penny	ship	time
low	pet	show	to
make	pigs	sit	toad
man	play	six	took
may	pup	small	top
me	puppy	smell	tops
men	put	snake	town
mind	rake	so	tree
mine	ran	stamp	tub
mitten	red	stand	up
most	ride	star	us
must	robe	start	use
my	ropes	stay	wall
name	roses	step	want
need	row	still	we
nest	run	stood	well
nine	sand	stop	went
no	sat	sun	what
not	saw	take	will
note	see	tape	wish
now	sent	tell	wood
on	shake	ten	you
pan	she	the	
pat	sheep	then	

You are a SUPER SPELLER!

Name

Congratulations!!

Answer Key

Page 21
1. at
2. a
3. am or an
4. and
5. an or am

1. John and Mary are having fun.
2. That is an fox.
3. That is a ox.
4. Look at that cat.

Page 22
1. am   4. a
2. and   5. an
3. at

Page 23
1. A
2. an
3. and
4. am
5. at

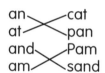

an — cat
at — pan
and — Pam
am — sand

Page 25
1. in or is
2. it
3. did
4. big
5. is or in

1. ni   (in)
2. (is)   si
3. (it)   ti
4. gib   (big)
5. idd   (did)

Page 26
1. did
2. in
3. is
4. big
5. it

Page 27
1. i
2. i
3. i
4. I, i

These words should be circled:
1. in   is   it   big   did
2. did   big   it   is   in
3. it   is   did   in   big

Page 29
1. pan
2. can or man
3. man or can
4. cat or sat
5. sat or cat

pan   cat
man   sat
can

Page 30
1. man
2. can
3. sat
4. pan
5. cat

Page 31

ran	rat
pan	cat
man	sat
can	pat
tan	mat

1. cat
2. mat
3. pan
4. can

Page 33
1. had
2. sit
3. as
4. six or ran
5. ran or six

1. as   as
2. ran ran
3. had had
4. sit sit
5. six six

Page 34
1. sit
2. six
3. had
4. as
5. ran

Page 35
ban   pan
fan   man
ran   tan
can   van
Dan

sit   ran
had   as
six   sit
ran   had

Page 37
1. fun
2. up
3. us
4. run
5. to

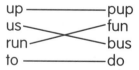

up — pup
us — fun
run — bus
to — do

Page 38
1. to
2. fun
3. up
4. run
5. us

Page 39
These words should be circled:
1. to   run   up   us   fun
2. fun   run   to   up   us
3. to   us   fun   up   run

1. fun fwn
2. yp **up**
3. rwn **run**
4. **us** ys
5. **to** tw

Page 41
1. pup
2. but or tub
3. I
4. tub or but
5. bus

pup	bus
but or tub	tub or but
pup	bus

Page 42
1. pup
2. bus
3. tub
4. I
5. but

Page 43

up	and
pup	can
run	pan
tub	man
but	had
us	cat
fun	sat

Answers will vary but should spell words.

Page 45
1. pat or put
2. sun
3. put or pat
4. dig
5. his

1. That is his book. his
2. I can dig a hole. dig
3. Please put the book down. put
4. The sun is hot. sun
5. You may pat the cat. pat

Page 46
1. his
2. sun
3. pat
4. dig
5. put

Page 47

as	is	up
cat	dig	sun
pat	his	but
and	sit	bus
man	it	run

1. cat   3. sun
2. dig   4. his

Page 49
1. not
2. the
3. on
4. dog
5. got

1. I like to run with my dog. dog
2. The cat is playing. The
3. Please get on the bus. on
4. I got a ball. got
5. That is not my cat. not

Page 50
1. the
2. not
3. dog
4. got
5. on

Page 51
These words should be circled:
1. the   not   on   dog   got
2. not   on   dog   the   got
3. not   the   got   dog   on

1. onn   **on**
2. tha   **the**
3. **dog**   dwg
4. **got**   gat
5. nawt   **not**

Page 53
1. red
2. fed or let
3. let or fed
4. get or pet
5. pet or get

fed	let
get	red
pet	pet

Page 54
1. red
2. let
3. pet
4. fed
5. get

Page 55

get	jet	let	met
net	pet	set	wet

1. fet   **pet**
2. **fed**   ped
3. ged   **red**
4. **get**   git
5. **let**   det

Page 57
1. men
2. fox or fix
3. top
4. stop
5. fix or fox

1. Please **stop** the car. stop
2. The **men** are running fast. men
3. Can you **fix** your toy? fix
4. The **fox** is in a box. fox
5. The fox is on **top** of the box. top

Page 58
1. men
2. fix
3. stop
4. fox
5. top

Page 59
hop mop pop top

Ben den hen
men pen ten

These words should be circled:
1. men fix fox stop top
2. stop top fix fox men
3. fox stop top fix men

Page 61
1. ten
2. sand
3. hand
4. hat or hot
5. hot or hat

1. ~~sand~~ sand
2. hand ~~hand~~
3. hot ~~hot~~
4. hat ~~hat~~
5. ~~ten~~ ten

Page 62
1. hat
2. hot
3. hand
4. ten
5. sand

Page 63

hen	pat	pot	band
ten	hat	hot	and
pen	sat	not	sand
	at	got	hand
	cat		

1. sand
2. pen
3. hot
4. hat

Page 65
1. bugs or tops
2. beds
3. pigs
4. tops or bugs
5. cats

1. (The cat was fed)
   The cats was fed.
2. (The pigs were fed)
   The pig were fed.
3. The bed were made.
   (The beds were made).
4. (The bug was eating.)
   The bugs was eating.

Page 66
1. cats
2. pig
3. bed
4. bugs
5. top

Page 67
(tops) uss (pigs) hads (beds)
feds (cats) thes (bugs) ons
(pig) fixs (tops) nots (bug)

These words should be circled:
1. tops beds cats pigs bugs
2. tops bugs cats beds pigs
3. tops cats bugs pigs beds

Page 69
1. ball or fall
2. bell or fell
3. hill
4. fell or bell
5. fall or ball

hill bell fell
ball fall hill
bell fell ball

Page 70
1. bell
2. hill
3. fell
4. fall
5. ball

Page 71
ball bell hill
fall fell

1. ball or bell, hill
2. fall
3. bell or ball, fell

Page 73
1. wish   4. ship
2. shell   5. dish
3. she

(ship)sh sh(wish) (she)sh
(shell)sh sh(dish) sh(ship)
sh(she) (wish)sh sh(shell)

Page 74
1. dish
2. shell
3. She
4. wish
5. ship

Page 75
dip, sip
fish, wish
bell, cell, dell, fell, sell, well

1. dish, wish
2. ship
3. shell
4. she

Page 77
1. make
2. lake
3. came or come
4. ate
5. tape
6. game
7. shake
8. come or came

1. ~~make~~ make
2. lake ~~lake~~
3. shake ~~shake~~
4. ~~come~~ come
5. came ~~came~~
6. game ~~game~~
7. ~~ate~~ ate
8. ~~tape~~ tape

Page 78
1. shake
2. tape
3. come
4. ate, lake
5. make, game

Page 79

ate	hat
make	sand
came	had
game	hand
lake	ran
shake	pat
ate	
tape	

1. make or lake
2. came or game
3. tape
4. make or lake

Page 81
1. ride
2. like
3. nine
4. by
5. five, dime, or time
6. my
7. dime, time, or five
8. time, dime, or five

1. five ~~it~~   5. ~~Dyme~~ time
2. ~~it~~ like   6. ~~dyme~~ dime
3. ride ~~Dyde~~   7. nine ~~Dyne~~
4. ~~Dy~~ my   8. ~~by~~ by

Page 82
1. nine, dime
2. ride
3. time, five
4. like, by
5. my

Page 83

dive	is
dime	it
like	pig
nine	big
five	did
ride	sit
time	six
by	his
	dig

1. five   4. ride
2. like   5. dime
3. my   6. nine

Page 85
1. rake
2. bake, bike, or hide
3. name or mine
4. bike, bake, or hide
5. fine
6. gate
7. hide, bike, or bake
8. mine or name

1. rake   5. mine
2. fine   6. bike
3. gate   7. name
4. bake   8. hide

Page 86
1. bike
2. rake
3. gate
4. hide
5. bake, mine
6. name, fine

Page 87

rate	as
bake	can
name	pan
rake	man
make	cat
came	sand
lake	hand
game	pat
gate	hat

1. gate   3. rake
2. nine   4. bike

Page 89
1. sheep
2. we or me
3. tree
4. he or be
5. see
6. me or we
7. need
8. be or he

sheep   be   we   tree
see   he   me   need

We see the sheep.

Page 90
1. be, tree
2. need, sheep
3. me, see
4. we
5. he

Page 91

be	pet
we	fed
me	red
he	ten
be	get
tree	let
see	men
need	bed
free	

1. me   3. tree
2. need   4. sheep

Page 93
1. you
2. note or robe
3. do
4. so or no
5. go
6. home
7. no or so
8. robe or note

1. yow   (you)   euw
2. (do)   duw   doo
3. roob   roub   (robe)
4. noot   (note) nowt
5. (home) howm   hom
6. nw   noo   (no)
7. sw   su   (so)
8. (go)   gw   gow

Page 94
1. do
2. go, home
3. you, note
4. robe
5. so

Page 95

no	hot
go	not
so	dog
no	on
home	top
note	hop
robe	stop
row	fox
	mop

1. so or go
2. note
3. home
4. robe

Page 97
1. use
2. gave
3. cone
4. snake
5. line
6. late
7. jeep
8. feet

These words should be circled:
1. snake gave jeep use line cone feet late
2. snake jeep use line cone feet late gave
3. use jeep gave snake line feet cone late

Page 98
These words should be circled:
1. cone
2. snake
3. feet
4. jeep
5. line

Page 99

long a	long e	long i	long o
late	jeep	fine	go
shake	need	bye	cone
lake	be	by	home
gave	bee	nine	
	me		

1. snake
2. jeep
3. cone
4. line

Page 101
1. ropes
2. boxes, foxes, or bones
3. bees
4. bones, boxes, or foxes
5. cakes
6. roses
7. kites
8. foxes, boxes, or bones

These words should be circled:
1. bones boxes foxes roses kites cakes
2. roses bees bones foxes boxes roses
3. bones ropes cakes roses bees foxes

Page 102
1. cakes
2. rope
3. boxes
4. kite
5. roses
6. fox

Page 103
1. bees
2. roses
3. bones
4. cakes
5. boxes
6. kites
7. foxes
8. ropes
9. fixes
10. lakes
11. notes
12. mixes
13. trees
14. makes

1. ~~foxs~~ foxes
2. ~~boxs~~ boxes
3. bones ~~bonees~~
4. ~~beees~~ bees
5. kites ~~kitees~~

Page 105
1, 4, 6, 8—went, sent, want, or mind
2, 5, 7—kind, find, or bend
3. ant

1. want
2. went
3. band
4. bend
5. bind
6. find
7. mend
8. mind
9. kind

Page 106
1. sent
2. kind
3. find
4. ant
5. went
6. mind

Page 107
1. find
2. want
3. wand
4. went
5. sent
6. send
7. mint
8. mind
9. ant
10. and
11. bent
12. bend

1. She ~~wint~~ to the store. went
2. He ~~sint~~ me a card. sent
3. I cannot ~~fined~~ my dog. find
4. Did you see the ~~ante~~? ant
5. There is a ~~beend~~ in the road. bend
6. Use your ~~maynd~~ to think. mind

Page 109
1. nest, must, or most
2. stamp
3. step
4. fast or last
5. must, nest, or most
6. most, nest, or must
7. still
8. last or fast

step	most
nest	last
still	stamp
must	fast

Page 110
1. step
2. most
3. nest
4. stamp
5. still
6. last
7. fast
8. must

Page 111

nest   most   step   fast
stamp   last   must   still

1. fast, last
2. must, nest
3. still, step

These words should be circled:

1. nest stamp must step most still fast last
2. still fast stamp last step nest most must
3. still stamp step most must nest last fast

Page 113

1. stay
2. day
3. toad or boat
4. may
5. away
6. play
7. coat
8. boat or toad

1. ~~stae~~ stay   5. ~~plae~~ play
2. ~~awya~~ away   6. ~~bot~~ boat
3. may ~~mae~~   7. coat ~~koat~~
4. day ~~dae~~   8. ~~toad~~ toad

Page 114

1. day, play
2. stay, away
3. may, play
4. boat
5. may, coat
6. toad

Page 115

In any order:
away clay gray
play stay tray

1. stay, play
2. gray, away

boat coat goat

You will need a coat to ride in the boat.

Page 117

1, 3—small or smell
2, 5–7—wall, call, will, or well
4. tell
8. all

These words should be circled:

1. small all wall call will tell well smell
2. wall will well all call tell small smell
3. all call wall small smell will tell well

Page 118

1. smell   5. call
2. well   6. will
3. all   7. small
4. wall   8. tell

Page 119

wall   ball   till
well   bell   fall
will   bill   fell
small tall   fill
smell tell

wall   well   will
sell   tall   tell
small smell pill
all   ill

Page 121

1. brown
2. down or town
3. cow, now, or row
4. now, cow, or row
5. town or down
6. row, cow, or now
7. low
8. show

cow   show row down
brown low   town now

We are now walking down the stairs.

Page 122

1. cow, brown
2. show, town
3. now
4. row, down
5. show, row

Page 123

pow	mow
cow	row
now	low
brown	show
town	tow
down	blow
how	grow

1. cow
2. show
3. town
4. row

Page 125

1. car or are
2. farm or harm
3. jar
4. star
5. harm or farm
6. are or car
7. far
8. start

car   far   farm
harm jar star start

The key would not start the car.

Page 126

1. car, farm
2. star
3. start, jar
4. harm
5. are

Page 127

are	can	make
farm	man	came
star	sat	shake
car	pat	ate
jar	and	tape

1. car
2. farm
3. start
4. jar

Page 129
1. little
2. funny or bunny
3. penny
4. puppy
5. happy
6. bunny or funny
7. mitten
8. kitten

These words should be circled:

1. penny puppy bunny funny
   kitten mitten

2. penny happy puppy funny
   kitten little

3. little mitten kitten happy
   bunny penny

Page 130
1. puppy
2. bunny
3. little
4. penny
5. mitten

Page 131
bunny   mitten   happy   puppy
kitten   funny   penny

1. kitten
2. bunny
3. puppy

penny   happy
mitten   funny
bunny   little

Page 133
1. then or this
2. lawn or fawn
3. saw
4. what
5. fawn or lawn
6. paw
7. law
8. this or then

law   lawn   saw   paw   fawn

I saw a fawn walking in the woods.

Page 134
1. fawn, lawn
2. law
3. saw, paw
4. what, this
5. then

Page 135
1. men
2. fawn
3. law or saw
4. brown
5. saw or law
6. now
7. row

fawn   lawn
what   then
law   saw
paw   this

Page 137
1. take
2. took, look, or book
3. wood
4. stood or stand
5. book, look, or took
6. good
7. look, book, or took
8. stand or stood

These words should be circled:

1. book good look wood took
   stood take

2. wood take stood stand look
   good book

3. took stand stood take wood
   book look

4. book look took good wood
   stood stand

Page 138
1. look, book
2. take
3. took
4. stand
5. stood
6. wood

Page 139
look   book   good   took
stood   wood   food   cook

1. stood, look
2. food, book

stand   band   hand   land
sand   grand   gland   bland

1. stand, band
2. land, sand
   or sand, grand/bland

Daily Language Review

Each book provides four or five items for every day of a 36-week school year. Skill areas include grammar, punctuation, mechanics, usage, and sentence editing. There are also scope and sequence charts, suggestions for use, and answer keys for the teacher. 128 pages.

Teacher's Edition		Student Pack (5 Student Books)	
Grade 1	EMC 579 978-1-55799-655-8	Grade 1	EMC 6515 978-1-59673-059-5
Grade 2	EMC 580 978-1-55799-656-5	Grade 2	EMC 6516 978-1-59673-060-1
Grade 3	EMC 581 978-1-55799-657-2	Grade 3	EMC 6517 978-1-59673-061-8
Grade 4	EMC 582 978-1-55799-658-9	Grade 4	EMC 6518 978-1-59673-062-5
Grade 5	EMC 583 978-1-55799-659-6	Grade 5	EMC 6519 978-1-59673-063-2
Grade 6	EMC 576 978-1-55799-792-0	Grade 6	EMC 6520 978-1-59673-064-9

Award-Winning

Daily Paragraph Editing

Editing practice targets grade-level skills from the language arts curriculum, focusing on capitalization, punctuation, spelling, and language usage. Each weekly lesson includes a 4-paragraph composition for students to edit and a related writing prompt. Also included are scope and sequence charts and annotated answer pages. 176 pages.

Teacher's Edition		Student Pack (5 Student Books)	
Grade 2	EMC 2725 978-1-55799-956-6	Grade 2	EMC 6551 978-1-59673-092-2
Grade 3	EMC 2726 978-1-55799-957-3	Grade 3	EMC 6552 978-1-59673-093-9
Grade 4	EMC 2727 978-1-55799-958-0	Grade 4	EMC 6553 978-1-59673-094-6
Grade 5	EMC 2728 978-1-55799-959-7	Grade 5	EMC 6554 978-1-59673-095-3
Grade 6	EMC 2729 978-1-55799-960-3	Grade 6	EMC 6555 978-1-59673-096-0

Daily Math Practice

Award-Winning

Grade appropriate, educationally sound, and designed to support your math curriculum. Based on NCTM standards, *Daily Math Practice* addresses key learning objectives including computation, problem solving, reasoning, geometry, measurement, and much more. Answer key and scope and sequence chart included. 128 pages.

Correlated to State Standards

Teacher's Edition		Student Pack (5 Student Books)	
Grade 1	EMC 750 978-1-55799-741-8	Grade 1	EMC 6527 978-1-59673-109-7
Grade 2	EMC 751 978-1-55799-742-5	Grade 2	EMC 6528 978-1-59673-110-3
Grade 3	EMC 752 978-1-55799-743-2	Grade 3	EMC 6529 978-1-59673-111-0
Grade 4	EMC 753 978-1-55799-744-9	Grade 4	EMC 6530 978-1-59673-112-7
Grade 5	EMC 754 978-1-55799-745-6	Grade 5	EMC 6531 978-1-59673-113-4
Grade 6	EMC 755 978-1-55799-746-3	Grade 6	EMC 6532 978-1-59673-114-1

Research Based

Daily Word Problems

Watch your students' problem-solving abilities expand exponentially as they experience the theme-based, real-world applications presented in each of the 36 weekly sections. Monday through Thursday contain a one- or two-step word problem; Friday's format is more extensive and requires multiple steps. All problems are grade-level specific, with concepts including addition, fractions, logic, algebra, and more! 112 pages.

Correlated to State Standards

Teacher's Edition		Student Pack (5 Student Books)	
Grade 1	EMC 3001 978-1-55799-813-2	Grade 1	EMC 6539 978-1-59673-115-8
Grade 2	EMC 3002 978-1-55799-814-9	Grade 2	EMC 6540 978-1-59673-116-5
Grade 3	EMC 3003 978-1-55799-815-6	Grade 3	EMC 6541 978-1-59673-117-2
Grade 4	EMC 3004 978-1-55799-816-3	Grade 4	EMC 6542 978-1-59673-118-9
Grade 5	EMC 3005 978-1-55799-817-0	Grade 5	EMC 6543 978-1-59673-119-6
Grade 6	EMC 3006 978-1-55799-818-7	Grade 6	EMC 6544 978-1-59673-120-2

Research Based

NEW!

Daily Academic Vocabulary

Daily Academic Vocabulary, the newest addition to Evan-Moor's popular "Dailies" titles, is a supplemental vocabulary series for grades 2–6. This series features direct instruction of vocabulary, shown to be the most effective way to expand students' vocabulary. Both reproducible teacher's edition and student practice book formats are available.

Two Great Formats!

Reproducible Teacher's Edition

- Definitions and sample sentences for each week's words

- Ideas for how to introduce the words

- Instruction that builds on students' personal connection to the words

- 32 Transparencies that display each week's words, definitions, and sample sentences

Student Practice Books

- **Days 1–4** each week present three or four practice items that focus on using the words in a scholastic or personal context.

- **Day 5** is a review that features four multiple-choice items and an opened-ended writing activity that requires students to apply the words to their own experiences.

- **Four quarterly review weeks** give students additional practice on the words introduced in the prior eight weeks. Practice formats include cloze paragraphs, crosswords, and crack-the-code puzzles.

Includes **32** transparencies

NEW!

	Teacher's Edition		Student Pack (5 Student Books)
Grade 2	EMC 2758 978-1-59673-201-8	Grade 2	EMC 6507 978-1-59673-208-7
Grade 3	EMC 2759 978-1-59673-202-5	Grade 3	EMC 6508 978-1-59673-209-4
Grade 4	EMC 2760 978-1-59673-203-2	Grade 4	EMC 6509 978-1-59673-210-0
Grade 5	EMC 2761 978-1-59673-204-9	Grade 5	EMC 6510 978-1-59673-211-7
Grade 6	EMC 2762 978-1-59673-205-6	Grade 6	EMC 6511 978-1-59673-212-4